MY PET
snake

Rennay Craats

W WEIGL PUBLISHERS INC.
"Creating Inspired Learning"
www.weigl.com

Published by Weigl Publishers Inc.
350 5th Avenue, 59th Floor
New York, NY 10118
Website: www.weigl.com

Project Coordinator
Heather C. Hudak

Design
Terry Paulhus

Library of Congress Cataloging-in-Publication Data available upon request.
Fax 1-866-44-WEIGL for the attention of the Publishing Records department.

ISBN 978-1-61690-082-3 (hard cover)
ISBN 978-1-61690-083-0 (soft cover)

Printed in the United States of America in North Mankato, Minnesota
1 2 3 4 5 6 7 8 9 0 14 13 12 11 10

052010
WEP264000

Photograph and Text Credits

Weigl acknowledges Getty Images as its primary image supplier.

Every reasonable effort has been made to trace ownership and to obtain permission to reprint copyright
material. The publishers would be pleased to have any errors or omissions brought to their attention so
that they may be corrected in subsequent printings.

Contents

Reptile Report

Snakes are a type of animal called a **reptile**. They have colorful skin and **forked** tongues. Snakes live in many different **habitats**. They can live in deserts, forests, grasslands, trees, and water. There are more than 2,500 different kinds of snakes in the world. Some snakes are harmless. Others can injure people and other animals. Over the past decade, many people have discovered the exciting world of snakes. These animals have become popular pets.

Snakes are cold-blooded animals. Their body temperature varies depending on the temperature of their environment.

Snakes require little attention from their owners. They do not need cuddling, grooming, or to play. Snakes cannot be taken outside for walks, and they only need to visit a **veterinarian** if they are ill. Still, as with any pet, caring for a pet snake is a big responsibility.

Snakes require care and love from their owners. It is fun to watch these amazing animals while they eat and hide in their shelters.

Hair-Raising Reptiles

- Many people are afraid of snakes. This fear is called ophidiophobia.
- The longest snake is the reticulated python. It can reach 33 feet (10.1 meters) long. The heaviest snake is the green anaconda. It can weigh more than 400 pounds (181.4 kilograms).
- The smallest snake is the Reuter's blind snake. It is less than 5 inches (12.7 centimeters) long.
- If handled carefully, a snake can be a fun pet for the whole family.

Pet Profiles

Snakes live in nearly every part of the world. Ireland and New Zealand are the only countries where snakes do not live in nature. All snakes are reptiles, but not all snakes look alike. Each species, or type, has its own appearance and behaviors. Some snakes have brightly colored skin or detailed patterns. Other snakes have solid colored skin.

Not all snake species are good pets. Some snake species are very dangerous. Many snakes produce **venom**. This poisonous substance can be deadly to humans or other animals. Other snakes are **constrictors**. They can squeeze a person or animal to death. Only very experienced reptile owners should handle these snakes.

Carter Snake

- Common snake found in North America
- Dark body with three light-colored, vertical stripes
- Grows to about 3 feet (91.4 cm) long
- Easy to care for and inexpensive to buy
- Some varieties have reddish coloring on their sides or spots rather than stripes

Corn Snake

- Lives in the southeastern United States
- Reddish brown with dark spots on its back and red and black checks on its stomach
- Grows to about 5 feet (1.5 m) long
- Calm and easygoing
- Lives more than 20 years
- Includes albino, orange, and snow corn snakes

common kinc snake

- Lives in North America
- Sleek black body with thin white or yellow stripes
- Grows up to 5 feet (1.5 m) long
- Breeds with other king snake varieties, including the California king snake and the speckled king snake
- Eats other snakes, including rattlesnakes

Hocnose snake

- Has a turned-up nose, which is used for digging
- Grows between 3 and 4 feet (0.9 and 1.2 m) long
- Uses weak venom to **paralyze** its prey
- Has large rear fangs
- Brown body with dark spots
- Many only eat toads

Boa Constrictor

- Lives in tropical areas in the Americas
- Yellow or gray body with dark patterns on its sides
- Grows to about 10 feet (3 m) long
- Easy to care for
- Kills prey by wrapping around it and squeezing it
- Varieties include tree boas and rubber boas

Burmese python

- Grows between 15 and 20 feet (4.6 and 6.1 m) long
- Weighs between 60 and 100 pounds (27.2 and 45.4 kg)
- Lives about 20 years
- Some have brightly colored patterns
- Common pets for experienced snake handlers

From Sea to Scales

Snakes are fascinating creatures. They have slithered around Earth for about 130 million years. Some scientists believe snakes developed from ancient amphibians called labyrinthodonts. Other scientists believe snakes developed from water lizards.

Scientists are unsure about the background of snakes, but one popular theory says that water-based mosasaurs are the snake's closest ancestors.

Scientists have found the **fossil** of a lizard-like animal that is about 100 million years old. This prehistoric creature had a light skull, long body, and two short legs. This may be the fossil of a lizard developing into a snake. Snakes survived when the dinosaurs died. As the years passed, different types of snakes developed.

Today, snakes live in many areas of the world. City gardens and wooded parks are home to small snakes. People can see dangerous snakes in tropical areas. More people in North America became interested in keeping these reptiles as pets in the 1980s and 1990s. Pet stores and specialty breeders sell snakes in nearly every pattern and color.

Run of the Reptiles

- Snakes and lizards are classified in the same **order**. They share many features. Some **skinks** and other lizards, such as the glass lizard, look like snakes.
- Reptiles and amphibians are different animals. For example, crocodiles are reptiles. Frogs are amphibians. Most reptiles lay hard-shelled eggs on land. Most amphibians lay their eggs in the water. Reptiles have thick, scaly skin. Most amphibians do not have scales.
- At one time, scientists believed snakes developed from lizards that dug their homes in the ground. Over millions of years, these lizards lost their ears and limbs. This change helped these creatures move around underground.

Life Cycle

There are only slight differences between the appearance of a young snake and an adult snake. For example, young snakes are smaller than adult snakes. Whether a pet snake is one month old or 10 years old, it still needs special care and attention.

Eggs

Most snakes begin life as eggs. Snakes mate in the spring. Soon after, the female lays eggs in a warm, moist area away from **predators**. She can lay as many as 100 eggs at one time. Snake eggs are soft and leathery. Baby snakes hatch from the eggs 60 to 100 days later. They use an **egg tooth** to break open the egg's shell. Some snakes stay in the shell for a few days until they are comfortable with their new environment.

Baby Snakes

Twenty to thirty percent of snake species give birth to live young. Each young snake is covered with a clear membrane, or thin layer of **tissue**. The young snake must break free of this membrane. Snakes that hatch from eggs are also covered with a membrane.

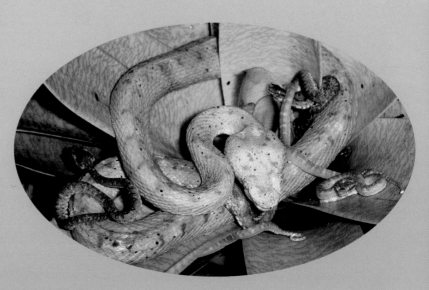

Young Snakes

Snakes grow very quickly. As snakes mature, they outgrow their skin. The outer layer of a snake's skin cannot grow, so the snake sheds its skin. Young snakes shed their skin more often than adult snakes. Snakes often live near their birthplace. Most snakes have a range of only 25 acres (10.1 hectares). Snakes return to the same **hibernation** dens each year.

Adult Snakes

Most snake species are fully grown between two and four years of age. Some adult snakes change their pattern or color as they mature. Some species become darker as they age. Others lose their patterns or brightness.

living life

- Snakes can live between 20 and 30 years.
- Young snakes are often more venomous and more likely to attack than adult snakes.
- There are no male flowerpot blind snakes. Females **reproduce** without mating.

11

Picking Your Pet

There are many factors to consider before selecting a pet snake. There are some important questions to think about before bringing a pet snake home.

Pet snakes often look very different from snakes found in nature. Breeders can combine different species and produce snakes with new patterns and colors.

What Will a Snake Cost?

Snakes can be purchased from some pet stores and snake breeders. Common snakes, such as corn and milk snakes, may be easier to find and less expensive than more rare types. When determining the cost of a pet snake, be sure to include the cost of housing. A **terrarium** and decorations can cost hundreds of dollars. Caring for a snake is not very expensive once these items are purchased. Still, owners need to buy feed animals, such as rabbits, mice, and rats.

Do I Have Time for a Snake?

Owners do not need to play with or walk their pet snake. Still, snakes require regular care. Owners need to make sure their snake's enclosure is clean. They must also check the temperature and conditions inside the terrarium often. Feeding a pet snake is quite simple. Most snakes eat only once every two weeks. Owners need to be comfortable feeding live animals to their pet snake.

How Do I Choose a Pet Snake?

First-time snake owners should select a species that is harmless, tame, and easy to handle. Species such as garter snakes and king snakes are easy to care for and make great beginner snakes.

Buying a Snake

- Make sure a snake is in good health before bringing it home. Look for cuts or marks on the snake's body. Make sure the snake eats well, too.
- Many breeders specialize in a small number of species. Buyers may need to search for someone who breeds the species they want to purchase.
- Buying from breeders is less expensive than buying from a pet store. However, shipping fees can increase the cost.

Reptile Home

A snake enclosure can be very simple or very fancy. It must provide everything the snake needs to live. This includes a water bowl, places to hide, and something to climb. A tropical fish aquarium makes a great starter terrarium. Wooden or plastic cages also make good shelters. The enclosure must have a secure lid. Snakes can escape through very small openings. It is very difficult to find an escaped snake.

A terrarium should always be at least as long as the snake. A 10-gallon (37.9-liter) tank could house a 24-inch (61-cm) snake.

Line the snake terrarium with newspaper or paper towels. These items are easy to clean and cheap to replace. It is important to have large rocks, logs, and sturdy branches in the enclosure, too. Snakes can climb on or rub against these items to help shed their skin.

Most snakes need a heating or lighting device in their terrarium. These devices heat part of the terrarium. The snake can bask, or lay, in the warmer area. Do not use hot rocks to heat a snake's terrarium. Hot rocks can burn the snake.

Reptile Residence

- Many people prefer to have at least a 20-gallon (75.7-L) tank for snakes. Pythons do not move much, so they can live in an 8-foot (2.4-m) long by 4-foot (1.2-m) wide by 6-foot (1.8-m) high enclosure.
- Snakes enjoy privacy. Be sure to place hiding boxes inside the snake's terrarium.

- Thermometers are an important part of an enclosure. Owners need to check the temperature as well as the humidity inside the enclosure.
- A snake will not shed properly if there is not enough humidity in its enclosure. Placing more water pans in the enclosure increases the humidity.

Snake Snacks

All snakes are carnivores. This means they are meat-eating animals. Pet snakes can eat mice, rabbits, or rats, depending on the size of the snake. Pet stores or supply houses sell snake food. Owners can feed their snakes mice they trap in their homes or garages. Snakes cannot chew their food. They swallow it whole. Snakes can eat animals many times their size. A single meal can satisfy a snake for days or even weeks.

Snakes digest their food very slowly. Do not handle a snake for at least 24 hours after it has eaten.

Snakes are fascinating to watch while they eat. Constrictors wrap around their prey. Then, they squeeze it. This does not crush it or even break the prey's bones. The snake tightens around the animal's chest until it can no longer breathe. When the animal is dead, the snake will swallow it whole, headfirst.

Venomous snakes strike their prey with their fangs. They inject them with poison. The venom paralyzes the prey. It also breaks down the animal's tissues. This helps snakes digest their meals. Snakes' saliva helps this process, too. Captive venomous snakes eat pre-killed prey. This prey should be frozen and thawed several times. This process also helps break down the prey animal's tissues.

Dinnertime

- Snakes have more than 200 teeth. Most snake species have two rows of teeth. Snake teeth point backward. This helps snakes hold their prey.
- King snakes eat a wide variety of prey, such as rodents, birds, amphibians, and other snakes.
- Snakes do not create their own body heat. This means snakes need much less food to survive.
- If humans ate like snakes, they could swallow a basketball.

Slithering Snakes

Snakes come in nearly every color and pattern. They also come in many sizes. Snakes may look different from one another, but they also share many features.

Snakes do not have movable eyelids. Instead, a clear membrane covers their  eyes. Snakes cannot look from side to side. They move their bodies to focus on an object that is not in front of their eyes. Snakes can see movement very well.

 Snakes have heat receptors, called pits, between their nostrils and eyes or on their lips. Pits allow snakes to "see" temperatures much like people see colors. Snakes use their pits to find prey, even in the dark.

 Snakes' mouths open very wide so they can swallow prey whole. The jaw can **dislocate** from the skull. The jaw can also open at the chin. This allows the snake to swallow larger animals.

Snakes have a **Jacobson's organ** inside their mouth. Snakes flick their forked tongue out to detect scents in the air. Then, they place their tongue on the organ to identify the scents. This tells the snake what is in its surroundings.

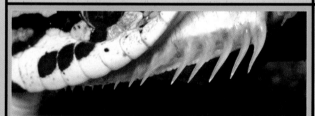

Snakes lose their teeth often. They grow new teeth. This means their teeth are always sharp.

Snakes' bodies are covered in scales that overlap like shingles on a roof. Snake scales are made from keratin. This is the same material as human fingernails.

Some snakes produce venom and store it in poison sacs near the back of their head. These sacs open into ducts in grooved or hollow teeth on the top of the snake's mouth.

Snakes can sense vibrations with the underside of their body. Snakes can sense other animals approaching by detecting the vibrations they make.

Snake Handlers

Owners should only handle their pet snake for 20 minutes each day when the snake is young. This allows the snake to become comfortable being handled. It also shows the snake that people are not a threat. It is best to make slow, even movements at the snake's eye level.

Smaller snakes are a good choice for owners who want to handle their pet often.

Handlers should hold venomous snakes with one hand around the neck behind the jaw. This controls the head and prevents biting. The other hand supports the snake's body. Large snakes need more support along their body than smaller snakes. Once the snake is more comfortable, it will wrap its body loosely around the owner's arm and hands. Handlers should always be aware of the location of the snake's head.

Constrictors should not be handled often. There should always be one person for every 5 feet (1.5 m) of snake when handling these animals. Owners should never allow constrictors to wrap around their neck, shoulders, or body. A snake tightens up when it is startled or frightened. This tightening can cause serious injury or death to the handler.

Large snakes, such as the Burmese python, become excited at feeding time. They may confuse their handler with the prey and attack. This is the most common cause of accidents with constrictors.

Striking Serpents

- Only experienced owners should handle venomous snakes. "Grab sticks "and tongs help keep handlers safe from a strike.
- Pet snakes do not often attack their owners, but it does happen. Pythons have injured or even killed their owners in the United States. Still, dog attacks happen more often than snake attacks.

- Snakes rely on their sense of smell to identify their surroundings. If owners have handled food, they should not handle a constrictor. The smell can cause a constrictor to become excited and attack.
- When handling a large snake, make sure an adult is nearby to help.

Healthy and Happy

Snakes do not often have health problems if they receive proper care from their owners. Caring for a snake is quite simple. Snakes need the right amount of food, fresh water, and a clean terrarium. Placing safe decorations inside the enclosure can help keep a pet snake healthy. Still, snakes can become ill. Snakes can suffer from runny nostrils, difficulty breathing, and wheezing if the terrarium is too cool. Turning up the heat often cures this problem.

Using the proper cleaning tools will help keep a pet snake healthy.

Pet snakes often have a problem with mites. These tiny **parasites** live near a snake's eyes and on its stomach. Mites survive by sucking the snake's blood. Mites do not often kill the snake, but they may weaken the snake. They can also increase the chances of the snake becoming ill with other infections. Pet stores sell kits that kill mites. The enclosure and decorations should also be cleaned to keep mites from re-infecting the snake.

Snakes can also suffer from mouth rot. Mouth rot happens after an injury to the snake's mouth, gums, or teeth. **Bacteria** enter a wound and start to destroy the tissue around it. Snakes with mouth rot will not eat. They will have cuts inside their mouth. A veterinarian can help pet snakes fight this infection. Without treatment, mouth rot can kill the snake.

It is a good idea to feed a pet snake dead prey. Live prey, such as rats and mice, may bite the snake, causing injuries. Owners should try offering dead, frozen prey to their pet. If the snake will not eat dead prey, clip hair from a live rat and roll the dead prey in the hair. Owners must supervise their snake if it will only eat live prey.

Clean Conditions

- To avoid **salmonella** poisoning, owners need to keep terrariums clean. They should wash their hands well after handling their snake, too.
- Pet snakes become ill more easily than those living in nature. In nature, snakes change their diet or move to a new location to make themselves healthy. Pet snakes rely on their owners.
- Water snakes may lack vitamin B. Feeding the snake frogs and salamanders can help cure this problem.
- Snakes can contract mouth rot by living in unclean shelters.

Snake Behavior

Snake species behave in different ways. All snake species share some behaviors, such as shedding.

A snake can have skin problems if it does not completely shed its skin. It is best not to handle a snake while it is shedding its skin.

Snakes will often stop eating before they shed. They spend a large amount of time soaking in water. After about three weeks, a snake's eyes become cloudy, and its skin darkens. After four weeks, the snake's face becomes swollen. This causes its old skin to crack open. Then, the snake rubs against rocks or branches to shed the old skin. It sheds its skin in one piece.

Snakes move quickly without limbs to propel them. There are four ways that snakes can move. Snakes push against the ground in a wave-shaped pattern to move forward. They can also use their scales and stomach muscles to move along the ground. They use their scales to grip the ground and move forward. Some snakes bunch up their bodies and then straighten out. This allows them to shoot forward. Some snakes lift their heads up and hurl themselves sideways. The way a snake moves depends on where it lives and its body type.

Pet Peeves
Snakes do not like:
- extreme hot or cold
- having no place to climb or hide
- being touched on the face or head

Shedding Serpents

- Some young snakes shed their skin every 20 days. Other snakes shed their skin only once each year.
- Many snakes hibernate during the winter. They do not eat or move until spring. Captive snakes do not hibernate because their enclosures are warm all year.
- The fastest snake is the black mamba. This African snake can race at speeds of 8 to 11 miles (12.9 to 17.7 kilometers) per hour for a short time.
- Some snakes coast through the air from tree branch to tree branch.

Snake Stories

In the Bible, a serpent, linked to Satan, tempts Eve to eat a forbidden fruit from the tree of knowledge. This results in Adam and Eve's removal from Eden and the loss of human innocence.

The Myth of Medusa

Once upon a time, Medusa was a pretty girl. She had beautiful hair. The goddess Athena was jealous of Medusa's beauty. Athena turned Medusa's hair into snakes. Medusa became a terrible monster. Any living thing that looked at Medusa was turned into stone. Using Athena's shield and Hermes' winged shoes, Perseus attacked Medusa while she slept. He did not look at her. He cut off her head. Perseus gave Medusa's head to Athena.

Many people are afraid of snakes. People have told tales and **myths** about these slithering creatures for centuries. Many stories show snakes as feared animals. The Irish celebrate Saint Patrick for driving the snakes out of Ireland. Snakes are evil in the Bible. Still, not all cultures think snakes are evil.

Snakes are adored in some parts of the world. Some snakes are religious symbols. The Mexican Aztecs worshiped the mythical serpent Quetzalcoatl. They believed he was the "Master of Life." Rock pythons are protected and respected by some African cultures. It is illegal to hurt or kill one of these snakes. The Aboriginal Australians believe the Giant Rainbow Serpent created life. Roman mythology tells the story of a god named Mercury who used his staff to stop two snakes from fighting. The snakes wrapped themselves around the staff. This staff became a symbol of peace. This staff is also the symbol of the medical profession.

Storied Snakes

- Some societies believed that snakes lived forever. This is likely because people saw snakes shedding their old skin and replacing it with new skin.
- People believed snake charmers had a magical spell over cobras. The charmer's song seemed to make the snake dance. In fact, the cobra was preparing to strike the snake charmer. The cobra swayed to follow the movement of the charmer's instrument.
- Author J.K. Rowling writes about snakes in the Harry Potter books. The young wizard Harry can speak to snakes. He also dreams that he is a snake.
- Many stories about snakes are not true. For example, some people believe that snakes have poisonous breath that can kill people. This helps spread the fear of snakes.

Pet Puzzlers

What do you know about snakes? If you can answer the following questions correctly, you may be ready to own a snake.

Q How often does a snake eat?

A A snake may eat once or twice each week. Some snakes do not eat for one month after eating a big meal.

Q There are two places in the world where snakes do not live in nature. Name them.

A Snakes do not live in Ireland and New Zealand.

Q What is the difference between young snakes and adult snakes?

A Young snakes are smaller and shed their skin more often. Adult snakes have darker coloring and different patterns.

Q What does the Jacobson's organ do?

A The Jacobson's organ detects scents in the air and on the ground. It serves as a snake's sense of taste and smell.

Q What should be provided in a snake enclosure?

A A snake enclosure should include a water bowl, places to hide, and something to climb.

Q How can you tell if a snake is preparing to shed?

A A snake may stop eating, soak in its water dish, and have cloudy eyes before shedding.

Snake Signs

Before you buy your pet snake, write down some snake names that you like. Some names may work better for a female snake. Others may suit a male snake. Here are a few suggestions.

Congo   Fang   King   Sissy

Slither   Hades   Viper   Copper

Roger   Patches

Frequently Asked Questions

Can I allow my pet snake to roam freely inside the house?

It is best to leave snakes in their enclosure. They are very quick. They can hide under floorboards and squeeze into small spaces. It is easy to lose a pet snake. They are difficult to catch, too. Large constrictors should never be allowed to roam free in a room with people. These snakes may attack suddenly.

Are there laws against owning pet snakes?

Many areas do not have formal laws against owning pet snakes. Some areas do not allow venomous snakes as pets. Owners need permits to own venomous snakes in other areas. Some threatened or endangered species are also protected. People should research different species to decide what type of snake best fits their lifestyle and experience.

How should I clean my snake's enclosure?

Owners should give their snake fresh water every day. The terrarium should be cleaned at least once each week. Lining for the cage must be cleaned or replaced. All the decorations in a terrarium should be scrubbed and disinfected at this time, too. Rinse all items very well to remove all cleansers.

More Information

Animal Organizations

You can help snakes stay healthy and happy by learning more about them. Many organizations are dedicated to teaching people how to care for and protect their pet pals. For more snake information, write to the following organizations.

American Society of Ichthyologists and Herpetologists

Florida International University Biological Sciences
11200 SW 8th Street
Miami, FL 33199

Society for the Study of Amphibians and Reptiles

Oklahoma Museum of Natural History
University of Oklahoma
Norman, OK 73071

Websites

There are many Internet sites devoted to snakes. To find out more, surf to the following websites.

King Cobra

www.nationalgeographic.com/features/97/kingcobra/index-n.html

Finding a Snake Veterinarian

www.anapsid.org/vets/index.html

Learn About Different Snake Species

www.kidsbiology.com/animals-for-children.php?category=Snakes

Words to Know

bacteria: one-celled organisms that can only be seen through a microscope

constrictors: snakes that tightly wrap around their prey to kill it

dislocate: to put out of place

egg tooth: a hard tooth on the upper jaw that falls off

forked: separated into two parts

fossil: the rocklike remains of ancient animals and plants

habitats: natural environments of animals or plants

hibernation: being inactive during winter

Jacobson's organ: a sense organ found in some animals

myths: sets of stories that explain a group's history

order: a group of related plants or animals

paralyze: to make unable to move

parasites: organisms that get their nutrients from living on other animals

predators: animals that hunt and kill other animals for food

reproduce: to produce offspring

reptile: a cold-blooded animal with rough, scaly skin

salmonella: a type of bacteria that causes flulike symptoms that can lead to death

skinks: smooth lizards with short legs

terrarium: a glass tank with a lid to house animals

tissue: a mass of cells that form organs

venom: poison produced by snakes to kill prey

veterinarian: animal doctor